Original title:
The Meadow's Muse

Copyright © 2025 Creative Arts Management OÜ
All rights reserved.

Author: Maya Livingston
ISBN HARDBACK: 978-1-80567-058-2
ISBN PAPERBACK: 978-1-80567-138-1

Murmurs of the Mellow Twilight

As shadows stretch and giggles bloom,
The crickets dance, dispelling gloom.
They sing of cheese, of pies awry,
Inviting us to laugh and sigh.

A squirrel with acorns on his head,
Claims he's the king of this twilight spread.
He gestures grand, in jest he roams,
A jester crowned in nature's homes.

A rabbit hops with floppity ears,
Trading tales of his past steers.
'Last week I found a giant leaf!'
He boasts while dodging playful grief.

With fireflies joined, a sparkling crew,
They light the scene with a twinkly view.
We laugh at puns, our spirits rise,
In this world of wonder and silly sighs.

Twilight Tales Told by Trees

In the dusky hours when shadows play,
Trees tell stories in a comical way.
One leans in close, with a creaky laugh,
Sharing secrets of a woodpecker's gaffe.

Oh, the oak with wisdom, often droll,
Claims its bark is what gives it soul.
It winks at the willows, swaying near,
'This trunk's not old, it's vintage, my dear!'

A birch whispers jokes in rustling leaves,
About a squirrel who always deceives.
'He hides his nuts, but forgets where,
Now he's on a quest, quite the affair!'

As twilight deepens with laughter shared,
The trees tip their boughs, all ensnared.
They paint the night with chuckles divine,
In nature's hall, where fun's the line.

Mornings Engraved in Gold

The rooster crows, a brash alarm,
He wakes the cow with quite a charm.
A squirrel struts with pompous grace,
Chasing his tail in a mad race.

The sun peeks out, a cheeky smirk,
While rabbits hop with joyful perk.
A dance of grasshoppers takes flight,
While bees hum tunes, all smiles, delight.

Sunsets Over Serene Fields

The sun dips down, a fiery show,
Cows gawk, wondering where to go.
A donkey yawns with half-closed eyes,
While fireflies gear up for the skies.

On bumpy paths, the turtle trips,
Then slides down banks with awkward flips.
As shadows stretch, the crickets play,
Announcing dusk in their own way.

Inspiration in Every Blade

Each blade of grass a ticklish joke,
That tickles feet as we all stoke.
A dandelion whispers secrets,
While ants parade in their bright fleets.

A wind gust laughs, the flowers sway,
A bee on a quest, lost on its way.
With every step, a giggle shared,
Nature chuckles, all well-prepared.

Harmony of Hummingbirds

Hummingbirds buzz, a feathered show,
With fancy moves, they steal the show.
One's stuck in a daisy, quite a sight,
As friends laugh at his flowery plight.

Dancing in circles, a nectar spree,
They hum and dart with such glee.
With tiny beaks and vibrant tails,
In their world, giggles never fail.

The Language of Lavender

In a field where purple sings,
The bees wear tiny bling.
A butterfly holds court, you see,
Making moves like he's on TV.

Whispers drift on fragrant air,
Bumbling bugs without a care.
They dance like they've had too much tea,
In this lavender jubilee.

Tapestry of Tansy and Time

Tansy blooms with a sunny face,
Stitching joy at a sprightly pace.
A dandelion makes a joke,
Puffing puffballs like a smoke.

Tick-tock dances with a fly,
As ants march on, oh my, oh my!
Grasshoppers ribbit with delight,
While worms groove, keeping it tight.

Serenade of Soft Skies

Clouds giggle, cotton candy spills,
Singing softly, giving chills.
A robin cracks a pun up high,
While raindrops wink and twirl on by.

Squirrels launch a daring chase,
Each leaping with a comical grace.
The sun grins wide, paints the scene,
As fields burst forth, so bright and green.

Rhapsody of Rustling Leaves

Leaves chatter like friends at play,
Rustling gossip in a breezy way.
A squirrel shouts, 'I'm on a nut!'
While turtles smile, thinking, 'What!'

The wind's a jester, swirling round,
Tickling petals that fall to the ground.
With laughter tossed on autumn's breeze,
Nature teases with such ease.

A Symphony of Swaying Blades

In fields where grass does dance and twirl,
The blades all play in a leafy swirl.
A concert held by the butterflies,
They flutter by with their silly sighs.

A rabbit hops, a songbird tweets,
Their harmony creates fun beats.
The daisies bow, proud yet shy,
As sneaky ants march on by.

Murmurs of the Wandering Wind

The wind whispers secrets, soft and sly,
It tickles the leaves, makes them sigh.
With puffs and poofs, it plays around,
Chasing lost hats that tumble down.

A squirrel's chased, through branches it flies,
While clouds above look on with wide eyes.
The gusts laugh loud, with a playful bend,
As twirls and swirls they happily send.

Portraits of Placid Moments

A turtle's slow and steady pace,
Paints a picture, a comical race.
While ladybugs, all spotted red,
Chase after dreams in a floating bed.

Sunbeams bounce, light tickles the grass,
While sleepy critters doggedly pass.
Every moment a canvas bright,
Filled with antics from dawn till twilight.

Canvas of Blossoms

Bright petals smile in the sun's warm glow,
They giggle as bumblebees gently flow.
With colors splashed like paint in a spree,
Each bloom declares, "Come dance with me!"

The breeze sifts through with a cheeky grin,
As critters whisper, "Let the fun begin!"
And daisies ask the trees to play,
In this jolly art, we laugh all day.

Aroma of Ancient Eras

In fields where cows wear crowns of grass,
The daisies gossip as they pass.
Old trees dance, and squirrels prance,
While bees hum tunes in a buzzing trance.

A whiff of history floats so clear,
A time machine made of lemonade cheer.
The rabbits spin tales of the days gone by,
As ladybugs chuckle and birds learn to fly.

So come take a whiff of this lively air,
Where whispers of daisies sway with flair.
Each flower's a jester, each stem a grin,
In this world where silly never wears thin.

With laughter erupting from every bloom,
The past holds hands with the present's room.
Nature's a clown, with colors so bright,
Join in the giggles, from morning till night.

Dreams Caught in Dandelions

A fluffball wishes on a sunny day,
Toss your dreams, watch them fly away!
The seeds scatter, a game of chance,
While kids jump up in a feathery dance.

A whimsy of wishes, with giggles galore,
They float like kites, seeking more and more.
Cats try to pounce, but they just float past,
Chasing dreams instead of mice, what a blast!

On the breeze, a dandelion sighs,
Transforming bids into cloud-traveling spies.
As giggles erupt, and the sun starts to dip,
Remarkable flights! Come take a trip!

So dream big, dear friends, as you send them high,
The fluff will tell stories to the evening sky.
With every seed twirl, a laughter-filled ride,
Sprinkling joy where the bright spirits glide.

Threads of Twilight Tied in Thorns

In the twilight hours, the thorns wear a veil,
As shadows dance, sharing jokes by the trail.
A prickly proposition, but the laughter's sincere,
Even cacti join in, with a spiky cheer!

As fireflies wink and stars start to hum,
A hedgehog wobbles, oh, where's it from?
With a pointy quill and a sense of delight,
It juggles those thorns, what a whimsical sight!

Threads of the dusk stitch jokes in the air,
The rosebush laughs while tossing its hair.
In this quirky garden, let silliness bloom,
As the bushes tell tales in the sweet-scented gloom.

So wander through twilight, with giggles galore,
Find the humor tucked behind every door.
With thorns in the backdrop, we'll laugh 'til we bow,
For every thorn's twinkle is a giggle right now!

Flourish of Flutters

In a fluttery frenzy, the butterflies play,
They waltz through the flowers, come join the ballet!
A twist and a turn, with colors so bright,
They giggle and flutter, chasing the light.

With daisies as partners, they sip on the dew,
Creating a melody, harmonious and new.
The wind hums a tune, and the grass sways along,
As the petals join in, a whimsical throng!

Oh, what a spectacle, this fluttering spree,
Even the ants join in, it's a sight to see!
With legs all a-tangle, they stumble and fall,
Laughter erupting, it's a dance for us all.

So come take a twirl in this vibrant display,
Where silliness blooms in the sun's golden ray.
In a flourish of flutters, stories get spun,
Where laughter's the melody, and we all have fun!

Shadows Cast by Sunlit Hues

In sunny patches, shadows dance,
A cat in glasses, lost in prance.
The squirrel's joke, a nutty pun,
While flowers giggle in the sun.

The trees debate on who is tall,
A dandelion's having a ball.
With petals as crowns, they laugh away,
As bubbles float through bright mid-day.

A worm in spectacles, quite debonair,
Slips on a leaf, gives it a scare.
The daisies hum a lively tune,
As shadows stretch beneath the moon.

So gather round and join the cheer,
In this green space, life holds dear.
With every chirp and leaf that flutters,
Laughter blooms, ain't nature's wonders!

A Canvas of Clouded Thoughts

The sky is gray but spirits soar,
As baby sheep start a woolly war.
In puddles, frogs wear tiny hats,
And giggle loudly, just like cats.

The clouds throw shade, a painter's dream,
With rainbows forming by the stream.
A lightning bolt's a silly prank,
While flowers roll in the soft, wet bank.

A duck's quack sounds like a joke,
As stormy skies begin to poke.
Each drop that falls, a laugh in disguise,
As puddles mirror the wet, blue skies.

Every bloom hides stories untold,
In this muddy mess, laughter unfolds.
So let's dance under this playful shroud,
Where thoughts are silly, and dreams are loud!

The Ballet of Butterflies

In a field, the dancers twirl,
With wings of colors that brightly whirl.
Each butterfly, a prima star,
Wearing nectar as glitter, oh so bizarre.

They meet to waltz, a grand affair,
With humming bees buzzing their flair.
Caterpillars wish they could join the show,
But they're stuck munching, moving slow.

The ladybugs, in sequins bright,
Clap tiny hands, cheering with delight.
As breezes laugh, they spin and glide,
In this whimsical dance, joy can't hide.

So take a seat, and watch the play,
Where insects dance without delay.
In the ballet of nature, laughter sings,
For every flap of joy it brings!

Trails of the Treaded Ground

The paths we walk, all zig and zag,
With muddy shoes, a number tag.
Each step a story, a tale to unfold,
Including mishaps, loud and bold.

The ants march like a tiny parade,
With crumbs of treats, they have it made.
A ladybug slips on a twig,
While laughing clouds watch, oh so big.

Silly footprints stampede in rows,
As the grass whispers all it knows.
Each wander brings giggles and grins,
Where every adventure, a new tale begins.

So stroll along this joyful spree,
Where laughter echoes, wild and free.
Every trail a chance to roam,
In nature's dance, we find our home!

Enchantment of the Evening Glow

In the field where daisies dance,
A rabbit tries to take a chance.
He hops and flops, a clumsy sight,
While fireflies giggle, oh what a night!

The grass tickles a thief's bare toe,
A sneaky fox lurks, but oh, so slow.
With a flick of his tail, he dashes away,
Leaving behind a startled jay!

A cow in the corner, munching hay,
Tries to moo in the funniest way.
Each note sounds like a trumpet's blare,
Making all the other critters stare!

With owls coaching the crickets' choir,
Silly songs twirl higher and higher.
The stars wink down at the lively cheer,
As laughter echoes, far and near.

Silhouettes Against Starlit Skies

Beneath the stars, a squirrel prances,
Lost in the music of moonlit chances.
A pig draws shapes in the cold, dark air,
While a sheep plays tag without a care.

The moon's a friend, a watchful gaze,
As frogs break into comical ballet.
They leap and hop with mismatched grace,
While crickets giggle in a leafy space.

A bear attempts to salsa dance,
Tripped by a vine, he takes a chance.
With a roll and a tumble, not so discreet,
He lands in a pile of fluffy wheat!

Together they laugh, a merry sight,
What a joyful, silly night!
As shadows prance in a carefree spin,
The laughter lingers as dreams begin.

Chronicles of the Chirping Chorus

At dawn, the birds commence their song,
But one off-key gets it all wrong.
With flapping wings and mismatched notes,
The others giggle as he proudly gloats.

A chipmunk writes, a first-timer's tune,
Singing to the sun and the glowing moon.
But all the critters can't help but stare,
As he slips on dew and tumbles in air!

A turtle joins with a slow, deep hum,
While a raccoon dances to a silly drum.
Together they form a wobbly crew,
Creating a concert that's not quite true.

With laughter ringing through the trees,
Joyful chaos floats on the breeze.
These peculiar friends, a quirky bunch,
Make music that truly packs a punch!

Melodies of Moonlit Meadows

At midnight hour, the frogs convene,
With warty smiles, they all look keen.
They start their band with a ribbit and croak,
As a hedgehog joins with a plucky poke.

A cat's meow mixes with the breeze,
It's a tune so odd, it makes one sneeze!
As owls hoot loudly, they all align,
Creating a ruckus that's simply divine.

The bumblebees hum in their sleepy flight,
While a fox struts boldly, feeling just right.
He twirls and spins in the soft silver glow,
Turning the night into quite the show!

With giggles galore, they share their song,
In the heart of the night, where all belong.
So under the stars, they sing till they tire,
A melody of whimsy that never grows dire.

Echoes of Solace in Green

In fields where daisies dance and twirl,
The butterflies flutter, oh what a whirl!
A snail on a journey, quite slow and grand,
With dreams of reaching the faraway sand.

The bunnies gather for a game of tag,
While squirrels argue, who stole the swag?
A toad croaks jokes, as frogs leap in cheer,
The laughter echoes, oh what a year!

The sun wears shades, just to look so cool,
As ladybugs line up, each a tiny jewel.
The grass tickles toes, in a playful spree,
While ants march in lines, oh so orderly!

The clouds are jesters, all fluffy and bright,
They play hide and seek, in the mid-day light.
As nature chuckles with playful delight,
We find our own joy, in the sheer sight.

Tread Softly in Daydreams

In a land where jellybeans sprout from the ground,
A cupcake tree grows, oh what a sound!
The rain falls as soda, fizzy and sweet,
While marshmallow clouds invite us to eat.

The dandelion wishes on a soft breeze,
A squirrel in spectacles reads with great ease.
A worm with a top hat, a dance on the lawn,
Keeps the rhythm while each flower's drawn.

Bees hum their tunes, with a beat oh so fine,
While ants play the drums, in a march line.
A hedgehog juggles acorns, what a sight!
Underneath twinkling stars, everything's right.

As daisies gossip, with petals so fair,
They blab about snails and the brazen bear.
With each little giggle, our worries take flight,
In a world full of whimsy, pure delight!

Glow of the Golden Hour

At dusk, the fireflies start up a show,
Belly dancing shadows, all aglow.
The sun melts like butter, so creamy and sweet,
While rabbits wear sunglasses, quite a treat!

A turtle named Ted steals a sip from the pond,
While flowers nod gently, of him they are fond.
The whispers of crickets, a lullaby tune,
As stars turn on softly, like a glowing balloon.

A dog named Louie spins circles of glee,
Chasing his tail, as happy as can be.
The breeze tells a tale of silliness past,
Of moments so sweet, like shadows they cast.

With laughter echoing, we bask in the glow,
Where silly things happen, in this evening show.
As night blankets softly, with twinkles above,
In the glow of the hour, we nestle in love.

Stories Spun in Silhouette

In twilight's embrace, shadows start to play,
A cat taps its foot, in a jazzy ballet.
The owl shares secrets with a curious mouse,
While raccoons set up their late night house.

Monkeys swing from branches, making a fuss,
While a frog on a lily pad sings songs with gusto.
The moon winks down, with a knowing face,
Telling tales of mischief, in a joyous space.

The grass sways to rhythm, when the wind goes by,
As fireflies blink like stars in the sky.
With laughter and giggles, the night comes alive,
In stories spun softly, where whimsy will thrive.

As shadows dance wildly, under a swish,
A bear breaks the silence, grumbles, 'I wish!'
To join in the fun, with a hat on his head,
Under the spell, of tales widely spread.

Hand in Hand with Harmony

In fields of green, we romp about,
The sun shines bright, we laugh and shout.
A bird sings tunes, so out of key,
Yet still, we dance, wild and free.

The clouds parade, with faces strange,
A bunny hops, but what a change!
It tripped on grass, a silly scene,
As friends, we giggle, mightily keen.

Stripey ants march like a band,
With tiny drums, they make a stand.
We clap along, they roll in lines,
Who knew ants could have such times!

The wind whistles a playful tune,
As shadows stretch beneath the moon.
With every riddle, nature shows,
That laughter blooms where friendship grows.

Caressing the Calm of Creation

Amidst the flowers of vibrant hue,
A butterfly lands, quite out of view.
It sneezes loud, the petals shake,
We chuckle softly, for goodness sake!

The river gurgles with all its might,
A fish leaps high, a silly sight.
It flops and splashes, what a fuss,
While frogs stare wide-eyed, causing a fuss.

A squirrel juggles acorns with flair,
But drops one high, plop! — straight in the air.
We howl with glee at its surprise,
As nuts rain down like funny skies.

The grasses sway with a giggling sound,
As whispers swirl all around.
In every turn of nature's play,
We find the lightness of the day.

Luminescence in Lavender Dreams

In twilight's glow, the fireflies pirouette,
With dainty sparks, a dancer's duet.
They bump and blink with silly flair,
As we chase shadows, with giggles to share.

The moon grins down, round and bright,
While owls hoot in a comical plight.
They twist their heads, as if in jest,
Trying hard to catch a little rest.

A sleepy cat sprawls, as if in trance,
It dreams of fish and a daring dance.
But off it rolls, much to our shock,
It lands right in a lazy rock!

Lavender whispers float in the air,
With every chuckle, we show we care.
In every corner of dreams that gleam,
We find delight in the light of a beam.

Whimming Waters Woven in Whispers

The stream giggles as it flows along,
A frog joins in, singing a song.
It hops and croaks, quite out of time,
While turtles nod, in rhythm divine.

We splash and play in the sunshine bright,
A duck quacks loud, what a silly sight!
With each little wave, we feel so spry,
A band of joy, beneath the sky.

The pebbles twinkle, giving a wink,
As fishes swim by, what do they think?
With bubbles bursting, laughter unfolds,
In watery worlds, adventure holds.

In whispers soft, the day concludes,
With nature's antics, we share our moods.
Together we bask in delight's embrace,
Creating memories, the silliest place.

Journey Through Emerald Fields

In a field so green and wide,
Bumblebees all take a ride.
They buzz about, a drunk parade,
On sticky threads, their minds just frayed.

The flowers dance in silly cheer,
Spinning tales we want to hear.
With every breeze, they nod and sway,
They've got the moves, hip-hip hooray!

A rabbit hops, a jolly sight,
Dancing bacchanal day and night.
He twirls and twists, oh what a show,
While daisies giggle down below.

Under the sun, a picnic starts,
With sandwiches shaped like funny hearts.
But ants arrive, they've brought their friends,
A party crash—where laughter ends!

Revelations in Radiant Blooms

Petals whisper, secrets told,
Of bees with swagger, daring, bold.
They zip and zoom, quite unaware—
They've crashed their bikes, oh what a flair!

A sunflower turned to strut and pose,
"Look at me, I'm fabulous!" it shows.
But winds so clever play a prank,
And twist its style, down it sank!

Dandelions puff our dreams with glee,
As wishes fly to lands carefree.
But they release too many friends,
Now every wish? The chaos blends!

A gentleman bug in suit so fine,
Tries to court a ladybug divine.
But awkward winks make her flee,
While he bumps into a nearby tree!

Heartbeats of the Earth

Earthworms wiggle through the ground,
With funky moves that astound.
They hold a rave, but all alone,
To beats of nature's funky tone.

Each heartbeat thumps, a bass so loud,
Bouncing critters join the crowd.
Frogs leap high, they croak for more,
While crickets tap upon the floor.

The grasshopper's dance, a crazy feat,
With springy legs and rhythmic beat.
He slips and trips but won't give in,
With every tumble, it's a win!

A wise old tree, it chuckles low,
At all this chaos down below.
Roots shake like maracas in the dirt,
"Join the fun, no time to flirt!"

Shadows and Sunbeams

Sunbeams stretch as shadows play,
A game of tag throughout the day.
The clouds are giggles, soft and light,
While sunspots dance—a silly sight!

A lizard winks, all dressed in green,
In sunlight's glow, quite the scene.
He poses grand, thinks he's a star,
But slips on grass—oh, my, how far!

The bugs march by in silly lines,
Repeat their steps, they draw designs.
"Oh what fun," they chirp with glee,
Until a bird swoops down to see!

At dusk, all creatures pause and laugh,
As moonside stories share and craft.
In shades of night, they reminisce,
Of sunny days and revelry bliss!

The Call of the Crickets

In the night, they chirp and sing,
With a rhythm that makes shadows swing.
Not a care for the moonlight's glow,
They're the life of the night show!

Each one thinks it's a rock star,
With a spotlight from a distant star.
But when the frogs start to croak,
They quickly change their tune, oh cloak!

The grass sways, joining the beat,
While the fireflies flash in their seat.
Crickets in tuxedos proud,
Performing for an audience loud!

Yet when morning comes around,
They all blend in, not a sound.
Now they're just a bug on a leaf,
Waiting for night without grief.

Dances With Dewdrops

Little beads on blades of grass,
Reflecting sunlight like a glass.
They twirl in a breeze so fine,
Inviting ants to join the line!

These dewdrops know how to party,
With moves that are quite hearty.
They jiggle and giggle in delight,
As spiders watch from their height.

A butterfly drops in for a spin,
Laughing as the dewdrops win.
Each jump is a splash, a laugh, a cheer,
Echoing nature's whims so near!

But as the sun climbs in the sky,
Dewdrops wave their last goodbye.
Fading into the day's warm glow,
Leaving memories of their show.

Reflections in the Rippling Stream

A babbling brook with a silly face,
Winks at the clouds, keeps up the pace.
It mimics the birds, makes funny sounds,
Chasing fish that leap from their bounds!

Tadpoles race like they've lost their heads,
While insects tap-dance on lily beds.
The water's giggle is quite a treat,
As it tells stories of its wild fleet!

Around the bends, the laughter flows,
Bouncing off rocks where the green moss grows.
Reflected smiles of the passing munch,
Make every splash a giggly punch!

Yet as shadows grow long and wide,
The brook takes a breath, sets aside.
Even laughter knows when to cease,
As the stars come out, bringing peace.

Colors of the Hidden Haven

A palette burst with shades of cheer,
Where daisies dance, with nothing to fear.
Butterflies play hopscotch in the air,
While petals giggle without a care!

Hidden creatures peek from their nests,
Curious of each other's quests.
A squirrel drops acorns, what a treat!
While bumblebees buzz a merry beat!

In this haven, the sun is bright,
Painting the day with pure delight.
Leaves whisper jokes in rustling tones,
Nature's laughter, a happy groan.

But when twilight starts to blend,
All the colors begin to bend.
As stars sprinkle sprinkles in the air,
In this hideaway, joy's everywhere!

Soft Serenades of Saccharine Silence

In a field where daisies dance,
The bumblebees may lose their chance.
With every buzz, they trip and sway,
Making flowers giggle in dismay.

A butterfly with quite the flair,
Wore socks and sandals, unaware.
The ladybugs threw tiny shoes,
As they waltzed in polka-dot hues.

The grasshoppers had quite a show,
Reciting tales that made toes go.
Their poetry, so boldly odd,
They had the blooms giving a nod.

When a squirrel scooted by with glee,
He waved at a cat up in the tree.
Now who knew nature could be such fun?
In this silly world, we play and run.

Play of Petal and Light

Underneath the sunny rays,
A daffodil starts telling tales.
The clouds roll in to join the tease,
As sunbeams tickle every breeze.

A tulip wears a princely crown,
Until a gust blows it right down.
It laughs and shakes off dirt and dew,
And joins the giggle fest anew.

The daisies join a line dance fun,
While ants parade, "Look at us run!"
With sandals made from bits of bark,
They twirl and spin, oh what a lark!

A curious owl, wise but tough,
Said, "Are we having too much fluff?"
But with a wink and a nod on high,
He joined the fun, not passing by.

The Spirit of Sweet Surrender

In the glade, some mushrooms grin,
With tiny hats, they spin and spin.
The fern leaves clap, they can't be shy,
As mushrooms jiggle 'neath the sky.

A rabbit hops in mismatched shoes,
Squeaking out some humorous blues.
He flips and flops with all his might,
And makes the flowers laugh outright.

The sunflowers stretch with pride so grand,
Waving back at a merry band.
They tip their heads, a perfect cheer,
For those who dance, they have no fear.

A grasshopper plays the merry flute,
While blooms shake petals, oh so cute.
In this lively, joyous spree,
Every grin is wild and free.

Breezes Whispering Through Bloom

Whispers float on breezy trails,
As dandelions tell wind tales.
Their tiny seeds on adventures go,
Sailing off in a silly show.

A crow perched on a branch so high,
Cracks jokes at clouds drifting by.
He caws out puns, so crude but bright,
The flowers roll in sheer delight.

A poppy pulls a prank or two,
Tickling petals, the whole garden goo.
The sun snaps photos of this charm,
As laughter spreads and causes alarm.

With each soft giggle, the foliage sneezes,
Birds laugh loudly, saying, "Easy peezies!"
In nature's glee, they sway and dance,
Creating a whimsical, lively trance.

Whispers of Wildflowers

In the grass where daisies grin,
A bumblebee forgot to spin.
He tried to dance but tripped and fell,
His buzzing laughter rang like a bell.

A dandelion, proud and tall,
Declared to all, "I'm not so small!"
But when the wind gave her a shove,
She tumbled down, a tumble-dove.

The clovers chuckled, green and bright,
They played hide-and-seek till the night.
They had a blast, but just like that,
A squirrel joined, and off they sat.

With twirling blooms and silly breeze,
Nature laughs, it aims to please.
So if you wander, take a pause,
Join in the fun, for there's applause!

Secrets Beneath the Sun

Underneath the sun's warm stare,
A caterpillar lost his hair.
He flipped and flopped, he made a scene,
While laughing at his lack of sheen.

The grasshoppers played a cheeky prank,
They painted rocks and sought the dank.
A wobbly frog caught in the game,
Jumped too high, yet felt no shame.

A ticklish breeze gave everyone chills,
As ladybugs crawled up the hills.
"What secrets hide beneath this glow?"
They pondered, while trading blow-for-blow.

The sun just grinned, its rays so bright,
As flora danced with sheer delight.
They giggled loud, oh what a fuss,
In nature's world, it's all a plus!

Dance of the Butterflies

A butterfly, dressed up in spots,
Said, "Watch me dance, forget the knots!"
With wings that flapped like crazy doors,
She twirled and spun across the floors.

Another joined, her colors bold,
"You think you're slick? I'll do what's bold!"
They tangled up, a comical sight,
Falling down with pure delight.

The flowers blushed, they cheered and laughed,
As petals ruffled in the craft.
The audience of bees applauded loud,
Two butterflies, so vibrant and proud.

So if you see them take a chance,
Join in, don't miss the chance to dance.
For in the air, with giggles rife,
Comes every little thing called life!

Songs of the Gentle Breeze

Through the trees the breezes hum,
Tickling leaves, oh what a drum!
With every gust, it sings a tune,
That tickles grass and makes it swoon.

A crow on high, he cawed and squawked,
Decided to join, so off he talked.
His voice was rough, his humor low,
But oh, the song—what a show!

The bushes rustled, whispers grew,
As perky ants began to boo.
"Get in line! You're off the beat!"
They laughed and danced on tiny feet.

Oh, what a jive, what joy they found,
In every pitch, a laugh was drowned.
So let the breezes twirl and tease,
In nature's choir, we do as we please!

Reverie of the Rolling Hills

A cow jumped high, wearing sunglasses bright,
It thought it could fly, oh what a sight!
Chasing butterflies, in a goofy parade,
With moo-moo tunes, the best serenade.

The sheep held a party, with snacks galore,
Baa-ing to the rhythm, they danced on the floor.
A pig in a tutu twirled all around,
While the rooster DJ spun beats, profound!

In fields of green, laughter took flight,
Silly creatures playing from morning till night.
With each little jig, and each gleeful leap,
Their merry antics made the silence weep.

Nature's Diary in Soft Whispers.

A squirrel wrote notes on a big acorn sheet,
About how the cat thinks it's such a sweet treat.
While a rabbit read tales from the grass, quite amused,
Of a mole who got lost, and was forever confused.

The flowers were giggling, such colors they sported,
Telling tall tales of the bees, they reported!
The wind whispered secrets that made petals sway,
As bugs had a meeting, debating the day.

A owl in the tree hooted jokes all night,
About mice who wore shoes, what a silly sight!
Nature's laughter rippled through every leaf,
As the critters all knew humor was their chief.

Whispers of Wildflowers

In a field of poppies, a bumblebee danced,
With moves that had all the daisies entranced.
They giggled and swayed, their colors ablaze,
As the sun made a spotlight for their wild ways.

The tulips held court, gossiping and bright,
About how the buttercups were out, fancy, and light.
A dandelion chuckled, just blowing away,
"It's my mission," it said, "to pepper the day!"

A ladybug slid down a thistle so green,
With tales of a snail who was too slow to be seen.
Amidst all the laughter, the petals took flight,
Sharing joy and ideas till the fall of the night.

Serenade of the Grasses

The grass blades started chatting, tickled by breeze,
About a shoe that got stuck in the dirt with such ease.
"Let's throw a bash!" one tall blade did propose,
And soon they were swaying in topsy-turvy rows.

A cricket recited poems with flair,
While the worms in the soil held a hide-and-seek pair.
The skip to the hop of a tiny ant band,
Made everyone laugh till they could not stand.

The wind brought confetti, seeds flying around,
As the grasses did jig on the soft, spongy ground.
With laughter and music, the day turned to night,
In this grassy groove, everything felt just right.

Dances Beneath the Dappled Sun

A squirrel in a tutu twirls with flair,
While rabbits hop, thinking they can dance like air.
The sunlight giggles, painting shadows bright,
As daisies shake it off, in pure delight.

A frog with shades croaks a funky tune,
While bees buzz along, beneath the moon.
The grasshoppers snap, keeping the beat,
While butterflies flutter, oh so sweet!

With each twist and turn, the joy spreads wide,
Even the ants join in, with nothing to hide.
A whimsical party, oh what a sight,
In this sunny spot, everything feels right!

So twirl and leap, as the day wears on,
For laughter and joy are never gone.
In this realm of fun, let your spirits soar,
With a dance in your heart, here's always more!

Secrets Beneath the Swaying Stalks

The tall grass whispers secrets, oh so sly,
While worms discuss plans for their big July.
A ladybug giggles at a tale so grand,
Claiming she's a knight in a tiny band.

The corn stalks sway, sharing jokes of old,
While the daisies tease, looking brave and bold.
In a patch of clover, a meeting's in sight,
As the mischief brews, preparing for flight.

A turtle with swagger walks by with pride,
Heebie-jeebies singing as they all coincide.
While fireflies wage war with their glowing sticks,
The mushrooms all giggle, concocting new tricks.

So listen close, catch the rumbles of fun,
In the sway of the stalks, where stories are spun.
With laughter as fuel, the secrets they weave,
In this winding world, you won't believe!

Echoes in the Emerald Glade

In a glade where giggles echo like bells,
A porcupine juggles, wishing him well.
The whispers of frogs carry tales of great glee,
As chipmunks stand guard, sipping their tea.

The willows sway, and the wind has a jest,
Spinning yarns of squirrels in playful rest.
While shadows perform, making shapes so wild,
Each echo a laugh, like a mischievous child.

A parade of ants marches, heels clicking loud,
On tiny young backs, they strut oh-so-proud.
The fireflies dance, flashing lights in the dark,
While crickets recite poems, hitting the spark.

In this kingdom of green, the fun never ends,
Bursting forth like a joke shared with friends.
So come share a giggle, join in on the lore,
In echoes of joy, there's always much more!

Lullabies of the Lazy Breeze

In the lull of the breeze, where the wildflowers sway,
A sloth sings softly, melting the day.
With each gentle sway, the petals all dance,
As they whisper of dreams and a lovely romance.

The dandelions tickle each passing bee,
As they snooze under clouds, so fluffy and free.
A hedgehog with style wears a tiny hat,
As he winks to the sun, can you imagine that?

The breeze strums a tune on the leaves all around,
While butterflies yawn, feeling sleepy and sound.
A chorus of crickets hums in the night,
As the moon joins the fun, shining bright.

So let your thoughts drift in this whimsical sea,
Where laughs mingle softly, as chill as can be.
With lullabies flowing, the world feels just right,
In the heart of this dream, under starlight.

The Heartbeat of the Honeybees

In a sunlit patch, bees take their flight,
Buzzing around with sheer delight.
They dance in the air, a quirky ballet,
Mixing their nectar in a jolly way.

With tiny legs covered in golden dust,
They make honey dreams with fervent trust.
But oh, what a mess when one takes a fall,
A sticky little bum, he's the star of it all!

Their waggle dance is quite the show,
Like a bumblebee disco, you'd never know.
With pollen in pockets, they sneak and slide,
Who knew bees could have such great pride?

So raise a glass to their sweet refrain,
To bees on a mission, never mundane.
In a world full of buzz, they bring the cheer,
With every little laugh, they conquer our fear.

Nature's Notes on a Breezy Canvas

The wind whistles tunes through the tall green grass,
A symphony played by critters that pass.
Squirrels mimic drums with a squeaky sound,
While birds hold concerts, joyfully unbound.

Sunflowers nod to the rhythm of day,
While daisies giggle in their own little way.
A butterfly flutters, a graceful diva,
With polka-dot wings, she's quite the achiever!

Even the ants have a marching band,
Parading through crumbs, they take a stand.
With acorn trumpets and leaf percussion,
Together they create a grand introduction.

Underneath the sky with clouds gallivanting,
Nature's own laughter is ever-chanting.
A wonderland busy, so full of cheer,
Nature's funny notes, let's hold them near.

A Soliloquy of Silence and Sound

In the hush of the woods, a leaf starts to crack,
A squirrel starts chattering, then quickly turns back.
A blossom declares with a giggly pop,
While silence is interrupted, then stops with a flop.

The frogs croak a tune, but can't find the beat,
Dancing in circles with froggy little feet.
An owl hoots his wisdom, a wry little sage,
In the theater of night, he takes center stage.

Rippling water giggles, as it tumbles on rocks,
While crickets compose their nighttime talks.
A whispering breeze passes a joke to a pine,
And all the forest chuckles, "Aren't we divine?"

A bug on a leaf, trying to sing,
But he's off-key, oh what a thing!
Nature dines on laughter, the receiver and round,
In the jumbled embrace of silence and sound.

Cacophony of Colors

Painted petals splash across the scene,
An artist's palette where laughter has been.
Red poppies blush while lilies giggle,
In the happy mayhem, they shake and wiggle.

Butterflies flaunt in flamboyant delight,
Spreading their wings, a carnival sight.
But watch out for bees in their race to compete,
In this hilarious hubbub, they think it's a feat!

The sunbeams burst through, a brilliant glow,
Tickling the wildflowers that sway to and fro.
And even the grass has a playful stance,
Doing the limbo, just waiting for a chance!

With hues intertwining, a riot unfolds,
In the colorful chaos, the laughter consoles.
Nature's own circus, bright and alive,
Where even the monochrome wishes to jive!

Verses Crafting the Calm

In a field where daisies sway,
Bumblebees dance, hip-hip-hooray!
Grass tickles toes, what a delight,
Laughter escapes, taking flight.

Silly squirrels gather for tea,
Chattering loudly, wild and free.
One spills honey, oh what a mess,
Nature's smile, I must confess.

Clouds roll by, wearing a grin,
Dancing with shadows, chubby and thin.
The wind whispers jokes in my ear,
Who knew nature could tickle so near?

In this spot, the world feels bright,
Each moment infused with light.
Joy bubbles up, a playful tide,
In this calm where chuckles abide.

Petal-Paved Pathways

Petals dance on a sunny trail,
A butterfly slips, oh what a fail!
It flaps its wings, a comic sight,
And lands on a hat—what a fright!

Caterpillars do a little jig,
Worms roll over, feeling big.
A ladybug joins, stealing the show,
With a tiny wave, it steals the glow.

Mice in the grass crack up with glee,
Watching the ants march, full of esprit.
A tumble from toad, oh what a thrill,
Nature's theater on the hill!

The sun sets low, laughter's still high,
With moonlit chuckles that float in the sky.
In this wonder, joy wraps around,
In petal-paved fun, peace is found.

Sighs of the Serene Surroundings

Crickets strum on strings of grass,
A serenade as moments pass.
Chirpy notes, a whimsical tune,
Laughter echoes, a merry rune.

In the dappled light, shadows play,
As butterflies giggle, swirling away.
A frog croaks jokes, with flair and style,
Its audience laughs, a little while.

Under the shade, a squirrel has fun,
Climbing and tumbling, under the sun.
It trips on a branch, what a sight!
Rolling around, oh what delight!

Serenity here, with goofy grace,
Even the flowers wear a bright face.
Nature's laughter fills the air,
In this calm, nothing's more rare.

Garden of Gentle Whispers

In the garden where giggles grow,
Leaves whisper secrets, soft and low.
A snail with dreams, so grandly fast,
   Challenges time—its limits cast.

Rabbits in coats, fashionista fun,
Strut their style, oh what a run!
With every leap, they cause a cheer,
   Hippity-hoppity, all draw near.

Twirling flowers hum a soft song,
As the day dances, sweet and long.
A breeze carries smiles, oh how neat,
With petals drifting, nature's heartbeat.

In this garden, joy does bloom,
Filling the air with laughter's perfume.
Serene and sweet, this place is bliss,
   In every corner, a light-hearted kiss.

Dreams in the Tall Grass

In grass so tall, a bugle beetle,
He plays his tune, a wiggly fiddle.
He hops and skips, a comical sight,
While dandelions cheer, with all their might.

A rabbit with a top hat, so grand,
Proclaims himself the king of this land.
He hosts a dance for all his friends,
For laughter is the rule, that never ends.

A butterfly lands on a sunny chair,
Winks at the bees and whispers, "Do you dare?"
They quibble and tumble, send pollen on a spree,
In this vast stage where all are free.

The grasshoppers tap out a lively beat,
While ants do the cha-cha, oh, what a feat!
They twirl and they swirl, with glittering grace,
In this whimsical realm, there's laughter in space.

Reflections on Dewy Petals

A snail in a shell, polishing bright,
Swishes his tail, says, "Oh what a sight!"
He gazes at roses that giggle and bloom,
As they rumble and tumble, making a room.

A ladybug flies with a swaggering glee,
Says, "I'm the best, can't you see?"
But slips on a petal, lands with a plop,
All the flowers burst out, laughing nonstop.

The dew drops listen, in their sparkling stance,
As bees hit the floor with a clumsy dance.
They buzz and they whirl, with nectar in hand,
Creating sweet chaos, just as they planned.

In this garden clip, where humor runs deep,
Even the roots share a chuckle or leap.
Every bloom is alive with a quirky delight,
Turning reflections into giggles and light.

Lullabies of the Golden Hour

As sunlight spills with a golden grin,
Crickets strike up their chorus to begin.
The grass sways gently, to nature's soft song,
While sleepyheads gather, it won't be long.

A squirrel tells tales of his nutty finds,
While the daffodils nod, oh, how kind!
They dream of adventures in shades of pink,
With sunbeams as crayons, they giggle and wink.

The twilight whispers, invites one and all,
"Let's rumble and tumble, answer the call!"
A toad joins the fray, croaking with flair,
His deep voice echoes, filling the air.

As night slips in with a blanket so bright,
The stars wink down, giggling at night.
In this serenade of nature's own way,
The lullabies play until break of day.

Echoes of Twilight Colors

In twilight's embrace, where shadows play,
A lavender poppy gets lost in the fray.
She stretches her petals, grabs hold of the wind,
Saying, "Watch me float, oh, where have you been?"

A firefly buzzes with plans to impress,
"This light show tonight? Well, you must confess!"
But trips on a leaf, lights flicker and fly,
The daisies all giggle, oh my, oh my!

The clouds drift by, in a cotton candy race,
While all the critters share merry embrace.
With a wink and a twirl, they gather around,
For echoes of laughter abound all around.

As day closes out with a vibrant flair,
Each creature finds joy, in dancing the air.
For every color tells tales of delight,
In this whimsical world, hearts take flight.

Paths Less Traveled

In a field of dandelions, I took a stroll,
Tripped on a rabbit, it stole the whole show!
Laughter erupted from bees in the air,
As they chatted and buzzed without a care.

A turtle in glasses was reading a map,
I asked for directions, he offered a nap.
'Get lost,' he said, 'it's a great way to roam!'
I pondered the wisdom, then got up to foam.

A hedgehog was juggling some acorns with glee,
While squirrels debated, 'What's the best tree?'
I joined their discussion on clouds made of cheese,
And left with a smile, my worries at ease.

Now I stroll with delight, and I often will say,
The path may be funny, but hey, it's my way!
So here's to the strolls where the sillies unfold,
In fields of laughter, let memories be told.

Whimsy Amongst the Ferns

Oh, froggy in ferns, with your top hat so neat,
You croak me a tune, with a tap of your feet.
A snail in a tuxedo slips right on by,
Says, 'Slow down, dear friend, enjoy the blue sky!'

A trio of bees made a band with some flowers,
They serenade daisies for hours and hours.
In twirls of the breeze, they are dancing with flair,
And I can't help but giggle, they don't have a care!

A family of mushrooms held tea in the shade,
With biscuits of butter that constantly swayed.
I joined them for laughter, their jokes were quite tall,
Who knew that such fungi could be so enthralled?

So here in the ferns where whimsy takes flight,
Life's little surprises are pure delight.
Each chuckle will echo, each chuckle will ring,
As I skip through this world, my heart's learning to sing.

Chronicles of Nature's Embrace

In tales where the trees hold secrets so grand,
The squirrels conspire, a comic bandstand.
They flip and they jump with a nutty finesse,
While pigeons unfold their grand stories of stress.

A cricket in shades threw a party one night,
Inviting the owls, who didn't take flight.
They danced on the leaves, while the stars had a ball,
Crickets sang loudly, a disco for all!

Now frogs wear bow ties, they leap with such pride,
Their croaks make a rhythm—it's hard to decide.
Are they crooning a love song or just having fun?
Either way, my friend, it's a night to be won!

So gather your friends in this cozy embrace,
With laughter and joy, let's welcome the chase.
For every adventure that sets us apart,
Nature's sweet humor will fill up your heart.

Sprites of the Evening Glow

As dusk paints the sky with a soft, glowing hue,
Tiny sprites start to twirl, oh, what a view!
With each little flicker and giggly delight,
They sashay through the shadows, charming the night.

A pixie in pink tried to ruffle my hair,
'Just a bit of mischief, don't take it so rare!'
The fireflies joined in, a light-up parade,
While I laughed at the game, oblivious they played.

The mushrooms gave warning, 'Stay clear of the pond!'
They gossip in whispers, of tales they respond.
But sprightly I skipped, their warnings ignored,
And found that the splash was my own great reward!

So here in the twilight where giggles unfold,
With sprites by my side, life's a story retold.
For every small wonder, each chuckle we sow,
In the glow of the evening, our laughter will grow.

Mosaic of the Meadow's Retreat

In the field where daisies blink,
A cow jumped high, it made me think.
A rabbit wore a tiny hat,
And danced around with a chubby cat.

The butterflies all sang a tune,
While bees debated at noon.
A squirrel tossed acorns with flair,
Claiming the spot without a care.

The wind chuckled through the grass,
As worms wiggled, they had sass.
A snail held court with a grand parade,
While ladybugs made a charade.

So here in this playful little scene,
Life is funny, serene and keen.
Nature's laugh is hard to beat,
In the meadow, oh so sweet!

Dreams Tucked Away in Ferns

In the ferns, dreams doze and snore,
A hedgehog moved in, now it's a bore.
A frog jumped in with a loud croak,
Chasing off the dreams—what a joke!

The dreams tossed pillows in a brawl,
While crickets giggled, watched it all.
One dream grumbled, 'I'll take a nap!'
The other shouted, 'No time for that!'

A butterfly zipped, playing tag,
While a sleeping fox began to wag.
Dreams tickled each other with mirth,
As laughter echoed across the earth.

So, in ferns, where chaos reigns,
Even dreams have silly strains.
Nature's comedy rolls on and on,
With every sunrise, a new dawn.

Legacy of Leaves and Laughter

Leaves gossip while fluttering down,
Sharing secrets without a frown.
Acorns joke about growing tall,
While finding shelter from the fall.

The branches sway to a merry beat,
A raccoon dances, oh so sweet!
Squirrels jest about the nuts they stole,
Making mischief is their goal.

In this leafy laughter fest,
Even trees join in—what a jest!
They rustle, whisper, giggle and play,
A humorous tale unfolds each day.

So raise a leaf to joy and fun,
In every corner, life's begun.
Nature's laughter, a timeless game,
In this legacy, it's all the same!

Reflections of Resilient Roots

Roots chuckle beneath the ground,
In their secret world, joy is found.
They tell tales of storms and rain,
And how they dance through joy and pain.

A worm joins in, cracks a joke,
While fungi laugh at the silly oak.
Together they thrive, strong and bold,
Embracing laughter, never cold.

Each twist and turn tells a funny lore,
Of windy days and what's in store.
Life underground is never bland,
With punny roots that take a stand.

So beneath the surface, joy resides,
In every laugh, nature abides.
Roots whisper humor, grounded and true,
A quirky community giving its due!

www.ingramcontent.com/pod-product-compliance
Lightning Source LLC
Chambersburg PA
CBHW071820160426
43209CB00003B/139